Contents

Acknowledgements
Thanks to George Bulman, National
Director of the English Volleyball
Association.
The publishers would like to thank the
International Volleyball Federation and
Rucanor for their photographic
contributions to this book.

 Rucanor

All other photographs courtesy of
BM Totterdell.
Illustrations by Ron Dixon of Taurus
Graphics.

Note Throughout the book players
and officials are referred to individually
as 'he'. This should, of course, be taken
to mean 'he or she' where appropriate.

Foreword

In 1954 I wrote a letter to the *Manchester Guardian* proposing the establishment of a British Volleyball Federation, an event which took place the following year. *Know The Game Volleyball* will thus be available in time for the fortieth anniversary of the sport's governing body in Britain.

Volleyball is played by men and women, by the young and the old, and by those with disabilities. It is played indoors or in the open air, and it is easily and cheaply organised. It is not surprising that it is now ranked as one of the most popular sports in the world.

Volleyball has versatility. Witness the fantastic growth of beach volleyball, particularly on the American continents. This book charts these changes and is thoroughly up to date. Simply and effectively, it will tell you what you want to know.

Don Anthony
President
English Volleyball Association

Introduction

In 1895 William Morgan, the Physical Education Director at Holyoake YMCA gymnasium, invented a game in which an inflated bladder was 'batted' by two teams over a rope. Morgan wanted a simple sport which would be suitable for a variety of physical types, both fit and unfit, and which could be played almost anywhere. This game served the purpose, and was dubbed 'volleyball'.

The game spread rapidly through the USA and elsewhere throughout the world. In 1947 the International Volleyball Federation (FIVB) was formed. In 1953 volleyball was introduced into the Pan-American Games, and it became an Olympic sport at Tokyo in 1964. It is now the top ranking recreational team game in the world.

The World Volleyball Championships take place every four years, and the five Continental Confederations hold their own championships every two years. Recently the FIVB introduced a World League, run annually, with the world's top 12 countries competing.

The court

Fig. 1 shows the court as specified by the FIVB. The playing surface is 18 m (59 ft) long by 9 m (29.5 ft) wide, including the outer edge of the lines. These lines are 5 cm (2 in) wide, and should be at least 3 m (10 ft) from all walls or obstructions.

A line 5 cm (2 in) wide is drawn across the centre of the playing surface separating the two courts. In each court an 'attack line' is drawn parallel to the centre line.

Two lines 15 cm (6 in) by 5 cm (2 in) and 3 m (10 ft) apart are drawn at the back of the end line to permit service from anywhere between them and the end line. The service area is a minimum of 3 m (10 ft) in depth.

The surface of the playing area may be sand, earth or grass for outdoor play, and wood or a composition surface for indoor play.

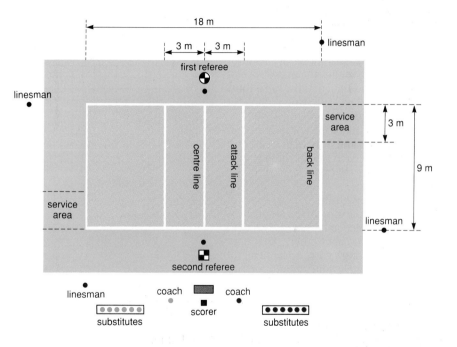

▲ *Fig .1 The court*

3

The net

The net is 1 m (3 ft) deep and 9.5 m (31 ft) long. It is made of 10 cm (4 in) square black mesh, and a double thickness of white canvas or linen, 5 cm (2 in) wide, is stitched across the top. A flexible cable passes inside the band of canvas, and stretches the upper edge of the net; it is essential that the net is taut, so that the ball will still remain playable if it rebounds from the net.

Two tapes made of white material, 1 m (3 ft) long and 5 cm (2 in) wide, are fastened near each side of the net, perpendicular to the side lines and the centre line.

Coinciding with the outside edges of the tapes, two flexible antennae are fastened to the net at a distance of 9 m (29.5 ft) from each other. They are 1.8 m (6 ft) long, with a diameter of 10 mm (0.33 in), and should extend 80 cm (31.5 in) above the top of the net. They are made of fibreglass, or similar material, and should be of contrasting colours, alternating in 10 cm (4 in) long sections.

The side markers and the antennae are considered to be part of the net.

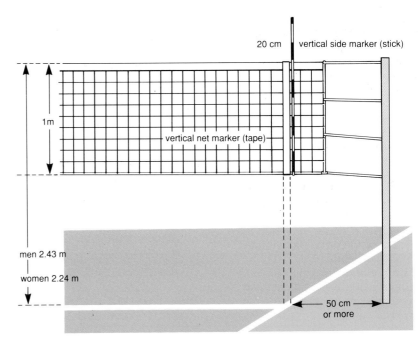

20 cm   vertical side marker (stick)

1m

vertical net marker (tape)

men 2.43 m

women 2.24 m

50 cm
or more

▲ *Fig. 2 The net*

Posts

The net is supported at each end by a post. The net must be the same height from the ground at each end, and not more than 2 cm (0.67 in) above regulation height. The regulation height of the net at the centre is 2.43 m (8 ft) for men and 2.24 m (7.33 ft) for women. The height for juniors and children is left to the discretion of national associations.

The posts can either drop into the floor or they can be fitted so that they slot into a base plate which is screwed into the floor.

The posts should be rounded and smooth. The side of the post nearest to the court should be free from any protrusions.

The ball

The ball is spherical, with a circumference of 65–67 cm (26 in) and a weight of 260–280 g (9–10 oz). It is made with a supple, laceless leather case, inside which is a rubber bladder.

When first starting to play volleyball, the choice of ball is important. There are a number of excellent purpose-made teaching balls which are ideal for beginners. These approved balls are lighter than their match counterparts, and can be obtained from the English Volleyball Association.

Do *not* use moulded rubber volleyballs. These sting the hands and arms and so do not encourage beginners. **These balls are not approved by the English Volleyball Association.**

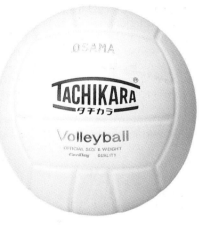

▲ *Volleyball*

Clothing

Members of the same team must appear on the court dressed alike. The players each wear a shirt or vest, shorts, and rubber or leather shoes (without a heel). It is forbidden to wear headgear or any other article, e.g. a bracelet or watch, which can cause injury to other players.

All players wear numbers: 15 cm (6 in) high on their backs, and 10 cm (4 in) high on their chests.

Clothing ▶

▲ *Shoes*

◀ *Protective kneepad*

Start of play

There are six players in each team, regardless of the circumstances. A team with less than six players automatically forfeits the game.

Choice of court

The two captains toss a coin to decide which team will serve first: the winner chooses either the right to serve first or the court in which his team wishes to start the match.

After each set, the teams change courts and the team which received service serves first in the following one.

Before the beginning of the decisive set, the referee tosses the coin once more to decide the choice of court or service.

In the last set, when one team has a total of eight points, the teams change courts automatically; however, the team serving at the time of the change continues to serve.

Position of players prior to start of play

At the time the ball is served, the players of each team must be placed in their own court in two lines of three; these lines may be broken ones.

The players nearest the net (nos 2, 3 and 4) are the front line players; the other three (nos 1, 6 and 5) form the back line. The numbers refer to the court positions (as in fig. 3 on page 8) and not to the players' numbers.

As soon as the ball is served, each player may cover any section of his own court, but the back court players may not smash or block at the net. The same player serves until his team loses a point. When the serve passes to the other team, the serving team rotates clockwise by one position before serving.

The rotation order must be observed until the end of the set. Before the beginning of each set, this rotation order may be changed, on condition that the change is noted on the score sheet.

Back court players

The rules prevent back court players from doing two things:

● they may not play the ball directly from within the attack area into the opponents' court unless the ball is below the height of the net
● they may not block.

From their own area, back court players can return the ball by any means permitted. A back court player smashing from his own area may land on or beyond the attack line (the 'spiking line'), providing his take-off for the smash is clearly behind the attack line.

If a back court player is outside the court but in the extension of the attack area, he is considered to be in this area.

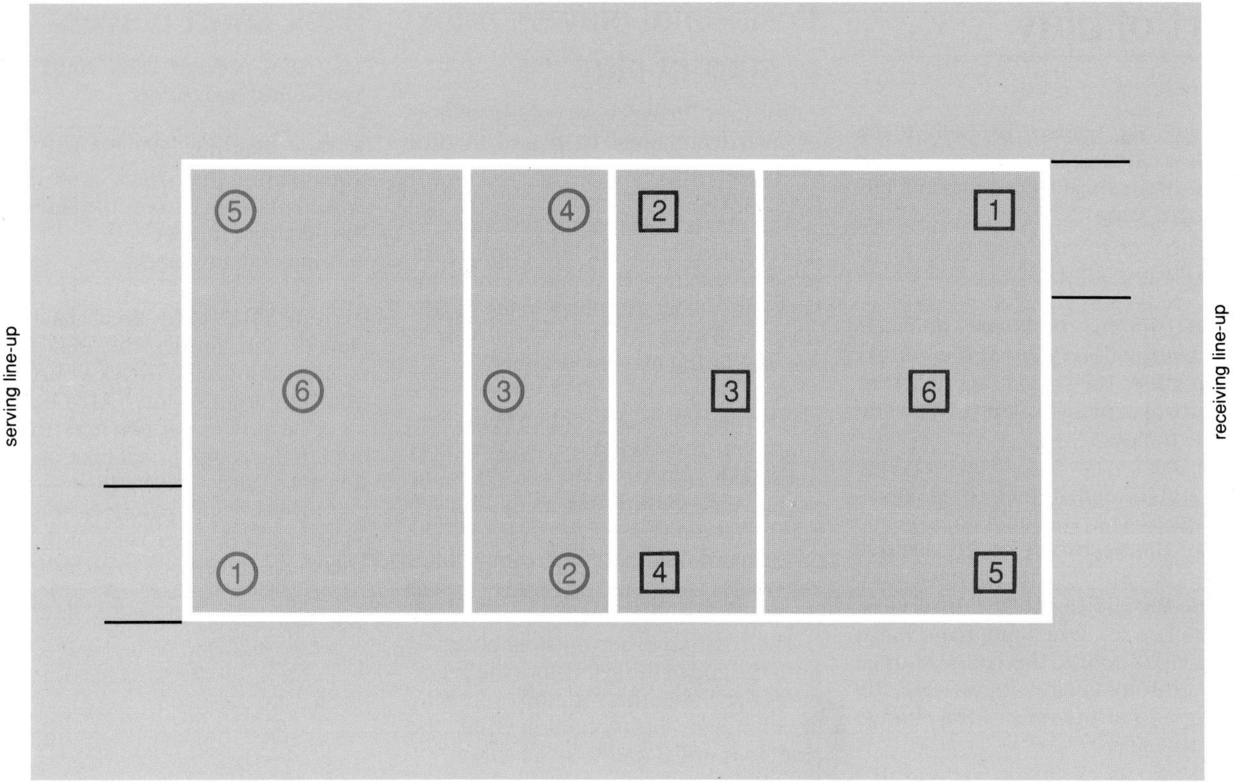

▲　*Fig. 3　Position of players*

The game in action

Play is started with a service by the player in position no. 1. The team receiving the service attempts to return the ball to the serving team's side of the net, using a maximum of three hits or less. No more than three hits can be allowed (with the exception of contact made when blocking), nor may any players hit the ball twice in succession (except if one of the contacts is a block).

The receiving team directs the first pass or service reception towards the net.

The second play is a 'volley' – when one of the receiving team volleys the ball into the air ready for the third play, the smash. The player of the team which smashes the ball attempts to ground the ball in the opponents' court, or to cause the serving team to misplay the ball. If this can be achieved, then the receiving team wins the right to serve, and so the chance to score points.

Except in the deciding set, only the serving team can score points.

Handling the ball

The ball may be played with any part of the body above and including the knee. A player who touches the ball or is touched by it when the ball is in play, is considered to have played the ball.

The ball can touch any number of the parts of the body down to and including the knee, on condition that this is simultaneous, that the ball is not held but hit, and that it rebounds vigorously. If a player touches the ball more than once with any part of the body, before any other player touches it in the meantime, he has committed a foul (a 'double hit').

The 'best' way of playing the ball accurately is with a volley pass. The ball must be clearly contacted; if it comes to rest momentarily on the hands or on the arms of the player, this is considered to be catching or holding. Scooping and lifting the ball are also considered to be holding.

Simultaneous contact

If two opponents simultaneously hit the ball above the net, the player from the team on whose side the ball does *not* fall is deemed to have hit it last. The other team then has three touches of the ball.

If, after the simultaneous touch, the ball falls on the ground *inside* the limits of the court, the team on whose side the ball falls is at fault. If the ball falls *outside* the court, the other team loses the point or service.

If two players of the same team play the ball and touch it together, this is considered as two touches (except in the case of a block). If only one player contacts the ball, it is considered to be one touch.

If two opponents make a personal foul simultaneously (a 'double foul'), the point is replayed.

The service

The service is the means of putting the ball into play. The player in position no. 1 (*see* fig. 3) stands in the service area, tosses the ball into the air and strikes it with one hand (open or closed) or any part of the arm. The server is not allowed to strike a ball resting on the other hand.

The server must stand behind the end line and between the lines limiting the service area. Having served, he may enter the field of play.

If the ball falls to the ground without being touched by the server, the service is retaken, but the referee must not allow the game to be deliberately delayed in this fashion.

The service is considered correct if the ball passes:

● over the net, without touching it, into the opponents' court, and
● between the two vertical antennae marking the width of the court.

The service ▶

The service is a foul if the ball:

● touches the net
● passes over or outside the side antennae above the net
● touches a player or object before going into the opponents' court
● goes under the net
● falls outside the limits of the court.

If the serve is faulty, the referee indicates 'side out', and the opponents gain service.

Net play

If the ball touches the net during play (other than the service) and passes into the opponents' court, it is not a fault. Even if the ball goes into the net, it can then still be played by any player other than the last one to touch it, providing that the maximum of three touches is not exceeded. If the force of the ball hitting the net causes the net to come into contact with an opposing player, this does not constitute a fault on the part of the latter.

If any player deliberately touches the net, he commits a fault. If two players from opposing teams simultaneously touch the net, this is known as a 'double fault', and the point is replayed.

Crossing the vertical plane of the net

It is a fault to hit the ball from within the playing space of the opposing team, or to cross the vertical plane of the net with any part of the body with the purpose of interfering with or distracting an opponent while the ball is in play.

It is *not* a fault to pass the hands over the net (with or without touching the ball) when executing the block or when the hands are inert, nor to cross the vertical plane of the net without touching an opponent or the opponents' court.

Passing the centre line

It is a fault for any part of a player's body to contact the opponents' court during play.

It is *not* a fault for a player to touch the opponents' court with his foot or feet, provided that some part of the foot or feet remains in contact with the centre line; nor is it a fault to enter the opponents' court after the referee has whistled to stop play.

Substitution

Each team is allowed a maximum of six substitutions per set. All substitutes and coaches must be at the side of the court, opposite the referee, either sitting on the team bench or in the designated warming-up area.

Substitutions may only be made when the ball is dead, e.g. during a time-out (*see* page 12), between points, etc. Each team is allowed two time-outs per set. If the substitution is not completed immediately, a time-out is awarded against the relevant team. If this team has already exhausted the allowable number of time-outs, it is penalised by loss of service or loss of a point.

During the pause for a substitution, the coach is allowed to advise the players. All players entering or leaving the court must have the permission of the referee, and must report to the scorer.

Any player beginning the set may, in that set, be replaced only once by a substitution. He may permanently re-enter the set only in the rotational position previously occupied. A substitute leaving the game may not re-enter it in the same set.

If a team becomes incomplete through injury to any player and if all other substitutes have been used, a substitute can replace the injured player even if he has already played in another position.

Time-out

A 'time-out' is a pause of 30 seconds for rest or substitution, or both. The captain or coach can appeal to the referee or umpire for a time-out when the ball is dead. Each team is allowed two time-outs per set.

If a time-out is utilised for tactical talks, the coach must address the players from outside the court, near the team bench.

Time-out for obvious injury is three minutes. If the referee notes an accident, the game is stopped and the point is played again.

Skills

Serving

Play is initiated by the serve, and it is an essential skill for playing the game. There are three accepted methods of service: the underhand serve (*see* fig. 5) is the simplest and should be used by beginners, but the overhand tennis (*see* photographs on pages 14–19) and jump serves are more potent in high-class play.

Good serving requires from the server consistency, accuracy and aggression. Spin can be added to all three methods by striking across and through the ball when serving.

Drills for serving

● The players are divided into two groups, and line up along each back line. Each player serves back and forth to a partner.

● A target is placed on the court (e.g. a towel or a hoop), and the serve is aimed at this target.

● The court is divided into various areas, with points for each area that is hit with the serve. Fig. 4 shows the usual scoring system.

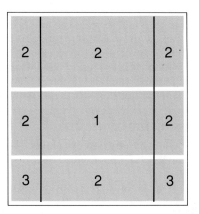

▲ *Fig. 4 Scoring system for a service drill*

▼ *Fig. 5 Underhand serve*

The overhand tennis serve

▼ *Before serving, concentrate, observe the opponents and choose the target*

The toss and the step with the left foot ▼ *should occur at the same time. The arm position should resemble that of a bow and arrow in order to accelerate the ball. Pay attention to tossing the ball low and without spin in front of the striking shoulder*

Before tossing, the ball should be a ▶ *comfortable distance from the body. The server should be confident*

◄ *Watch the ball. Keep the wrist rigid and the hand flat, but keep the forearm and shoulder relaxed – this maximises ball acceleration*

The weight is transferred to the front foot. ▶
The striking shoulder is rotated high as the hand moves away from the ball

◄ *Lead with the elbow – it is the key to the rate of forearm acceleration. The power originates in the hip rotation, and moves to the back, the shoulder, the elbow and the hand. The palm should point towards the ceiling. The swing of the arm should be horizontal, i.e. parallel to the floor*

Accelerate the arm on contact. When the ▶ arm swing is close to the ball (two ball widths), accelerate suddenly towards the ball. Maximum acceleration = maximum power

▼ *The best contact point for the overhand* ▼ *tennis serve is the base of the palm. Attention must be paid to making contact through the centre of the ball*

▲ *Directing the serve: the striking point on the ball must be aligned with the striking shoulder; the server's step and toe must be in the direction of the target; the follow through must be in the direction of the target*

▲ *Concentration is intense. The right hand is rigid and flat. The base of the palm touches the ball to reinforce the contact point*

Whip motion: the striking shoulder and ▶ *the chest are spread open; the elbow is back and the right hip is in a good position to begin rotating forwards to create force through the upper body towards the arm swing*

▲ *The elbow leads the forearm acceleration. The rigid and flat hand has remained with the palm towards the ceiling. This motion is similar to the last action of a tennis serve*

▲ *The serving motion is different from that of smashing in that the shoulder is not extended and the wrist does not break downwards*

Setting

Setting uses the two-handed volley technique to keep the ball in play, to set up an attack or to pass the ball over the net. The photographs starting on page 20 show the player setting up an attack.

Drills for the volley

One ball per player
● Toss the ball high and let it bounce. Anticipate where the ball is going. Move under it and volley it to yourself.
● Volley the ball overhead repetitively.
● The height of the ball is altered: high and low. Use knee extension to control the height of the ball.
● Volley overhead; volley forwards two or three steps; move under the ball; volley overhead; volley back. Repeat.
● Standing 60–90 cm (24–36 in) from a wall, volley the ball against it. Repeat the drill at a distance of 3 m (10 ft) from the wall.

One ball, two players
● The ball is volleyed back and forth, varying the distance between the partners.
● The drill is as above, with a deep knee bend and a jump (or any other callisthenic movement) between the volleys.
● The first player volleys the ball and then jumps, sits, bends or makes another movement; the second player must mirror this movement when he has volleyed the ball.

▲ Setters must possess quick judgement and movement, perfect hand position and good athletic ability

▲ While moving, watch the ball intensely. Also observe receivers and the approach of hitters

▲ *Penetrate quickly on a curve close to the net. Keep the body open, facing towards the receivers. Stop with a slide step on a position 30 cm (12 in) from the centre line and 3–4 m (10–13 ft) from the side line*

▲ *Make sure you are balanced. The right foot is forwards, the hands are high and the fingers are open. Keep the ball in front of the forehead*

▲ *Before setting, cup the hands on contact. The index and middle fingers are open, and the thumb is on the bottom of the ball. The ring and small fingers help to control direction*

▲ *For accuracy, make sure you are stable and square to the target. Extend the knees and elbows up through the ball. Transfer your weight from the back to the front*

▲ *For the high set: extend the elbows; soften the control with the wrists and the fingers; point the fingers towards the target*

◀ Get the body under a low pass. Use a deep squat body position, with the right foot forwards. When it is not possible to position the body under the ball, use the underhand pass to set the ball. Keep the arms straight, and the ball is set away from the net to ensure that the smasher has room in which to operate. For a set over a short distance, the fingers and the wrist flick the ball. Use minimal elbow extension – this makes it difficult for opponents to anticipate. For a set over a long distance, you must use the whole body. The entire body weight must be co-ordinated through the ball in the direction of the target. For the 'reverse' set, keep the ball above the head with the palm towards the ceiling while setting. Arch the back and follow through with the hands towards the target

▲ For the flat set: keep the hands high; press forwards the upper body, the forearm and the hands. Different sets require different techniques

▲ *Hand formation: triangle. Spread the elbows, though not too wide. Bend the elbow joint at 90°. Look through the enlarged triangle*

▲ *Contact the ball above the forehead. Relax the forearms but keep the fingers strong*

Group drills

● The players are in two lines facing each other, and the ball is passed back and forth. After a player passes the ball, he goes to the back of the other group (*see* fig. 6).

● As above, but the ball is volleyed over the net.

● Two players (X1 and X2) each have a ball. X1 volleys his ball to X3, who returns it with a volley. X3 moves to a marker in front of X2, who volleys to that position, X2 volleys it back, and returns to the original position. The drill is repeated 20–30 times.

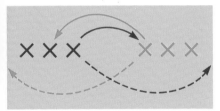

▲ *Fig. 6 Group drill for the volley*

Passing

The dig, or two-handed underhand pass, is used to receive serve or to pass a ball that is too low or too powerful to be volleyed.

Drills for the dig

One ball, two players

● One player feeds the ball to his partner, who digs it back. Change places after 10–15 repetitions.

● As above, but the receiver must come forwards to play the ball. He then moves back to his original position, and the drill is repeated.

One ball per player

● The player digs the ball repeatedly overhead, keeping the ball under control. Use a knee extension, not an arm swing, to control the ball.

● As above, but the height is altered: high and low.

▼ Establish the ready position: the feet are apart, slightly wider than shoulder width; the knees are bent and the hips are low; the back is parallel to the shins; the arms are in front and relaxed

◄ During contact, keep the arms together, the elbows locked and the hands pointing downwards. The arms should make contact on the fleshy part of their inner sides for a good rebound

▲ Move early and get behind the ball. Establish a low body position, with the legs flexed. Keep the arms relaxed and away from the body at roughly a 45° angle to the floor

▲ During the passing movement, shrug the shoulders, don't stretch them. The back foot will be raised as the legs are extended. The weight will move through the ball in the direction of the intended target. Don't swing the arms at the ball, extend the knees or use the body weight to dig the ball

▲ The ball must be kept in front of the body and between the feet. Always try to face the target. If the target is on the right side of the court, attempt to plant the left foot first in order to transfer your weight on to the right foot in the direction of the target

▲ Every coach should check the individual technique of the passer, and not allow improper contact

▼ *Lock the hands. The space between the arms is minimal (touching if possible). The contact point is approximately 5–12 cm (2–5 in) above the wrist and on the inside part of the forearms. One hand must be placed inside the other with the heels of the hands together. The fingers overlap, with the right thumb locking on to the first section of the left middle finger*

Smashing

The smash is the chief offensive weapon in volleyball, and consists of hitting the ball downwards, at great speed, towards the opponents' court. It is one of the most difficult skills in the game, but it is the most satisfying from the point of view of both the player and the spectator.

Drills for the smash

Hitting a stationary ball

The coach stands on a chair or table and holds the ball close to the net and above it. (The net may be lowered below regulation height for training.) The player uses the approach steps, takes off and hits the ball out of the coach's hand down into the opposite court.

▲ Stand at least 3 m (10 ft) from the net in a medium high position about 1 m (3 ft) outside the court. Begin with a short right lead step towards the attack area. Focus on the ball and lean the body slightly towards the net. You must be aggressive and full of confidence

▲ The second step, with the left foot, is a little longer. The weight is transferred to the left foot in preparation for the explosive hop to the ball. The arms are in position to begin the swing backwards

◀ *The arms have swung forcefully forwards and down. The knees are bent and ready to extend and push off*

▲ *The approach is adjusted in the final hop to a position below and behind the ball. Speed is gathered with a quick, explosive stride step. The heel is planted to slow forward momentum. The arms are at an angle of 90° behind the body*

Both toes leave the ground simultaneously ▶ *as the ankles extend and push off the ground. The striking (right) arm begins to pull back like a bow and arrow, while the left arm points at the ball. The right hip is open to begin the rotation forwards for the smashing motion*

▼ The shoulder is spread and stretched back as the elbow remains high. The hip rotates forwards to initiate the swing. The left arm drops down to help maintain balance

For the line smash, rotate the shoulders ▶ across the body towards the target. Rotate the striking hand up and over the ball, and extend the wrist down. Follow through with the arm down towards the navel

Force is applied upwards from the hip to ▶ the back, shoulder, elbow and wrist. The right hand has moved back and the elbow forwards as the whip-like action begins. Point the palm towards the ceiling

◀ The shoulder reaches and the arm extends straight as the ball is contacted in front of the striking shoulder. The striking hand is rotated outwards for the angled smash. Use a piking motion with the stomach to generate power

The elbow extends fully as the ball is ▶ contacted above and in front of the striking shoulder. The wrist extends up and over the ball. Keep the eyes focused on the centre of the ball

▼ The shoulder is stretched up and forwards during the follow through. For the angled smash, the wrist whips from inside to outside

▲ Ball contact: the wrist extends up and over; the contact point is at the base of the hand to the palm and to the fingers; the fingers are spread wide for control

▲ For the angled smash, the follow through is outside the plane of the body. The legs have recoiled and are ready for landing. Follow the ball with your eyes

▲ The shoulder rotates forwards and up towards the ball. The elbow follows the shoulder and remains high. The hand is back, with the palm towards the ceiling

▲ *For the angled smash, the follow through continues outside the plane of the body. The left arm has moved down and towards the body to maintain balance. Your eyes should follow the ball*

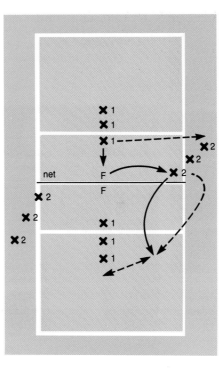

◀ *Fig. 7 Group drill for the smash*

Hitting a tossed ball

● One ball, one player: once a player acquires the ability to hit a held ball, the coach tosses the ball in the air while standing close to the net. The ball should go at least 3 m (10 ft) above the top of the net.

● Group drill (*see* fig. 7): a player passes the ball to one of the feeders (F), and then joins the line-up to smash. After smashing, the player goes round the post, retrieves a ball and joins the line on the other side of the net. For the drill to work, players must run continuously to retrieve the balls.

Blocking

Blocking is the defensive counter move to the smash. In order to block, the player jumps into the air and stretches his arms out above him. The block can be played by all three players in the front line, but it is usually played by just two.

If the ball touches one or more players taking part in a block, only one touch is counted. Any player who has blocked may then play the ball as a second touch.

Blockers may pass their hands over the net to meet any ball on the opponent's side of the net which is being attacked, even if it is not the third hit.

Drills for blocking

One ball, two players

● The net should be lowered to make it easy for players to reach over it with a slight jump. Two players stand on opposite sides of the net. The first player tosses the ball at a point just above the net and in front of his partner. The partner jumps, puts his hands over the net and pushes the ball towards the floor. The drill is repeated ten times, and the players then change around.

● The drill is practised as above, with the following variation: the player with the ball jumps in the air to smash, tossing the ball with his non-smashing hand. The other player jumps to block.

● A blocking drill is incorporated with one of the smashing drills.

▲ *Ready position: hands high, knees slightly bent and ready to move; feet shoulder width apart; body an upper arm's distance from the net, with the shoulders parallel to the net*

▲ *After moving to this position, read the attack patterns and be ready to jump. Focus the eyes on the setter's hands. For a quick attack, the hands must remain high*

33

▲ *The arms 'seal' the net as the blocker reaches for the ball. The head is still straight, with the eyes focused on the hitter. The entire arm movement should be one fluid move for quick penetration*

▲ *The knees and elbows begin to extend as the ankles push off the ground. The shoulders remain parallel to the net. The arms should always remain in front of the body and face, not to the side*

▲ *The arms and hands are less than a ball's width apart. The wrists are pressed down to deflect the ball to the ground. The arms are as close to the net as possible*

▲ Sequence of eye movement when blocking: hitter → setter → ball → hitter. The eyes have moved from the hitter and are now focused on the setter. The hands are shoulder height and in front of the body close to the net. They are forward and strong, not back and soft. The fingers and thumbs are spread, as if ready to play the piano

▲ The two blockers' hands are high and their eyes are focused on the approach. The outside blocker 'sets' block and is ready to jump. He keeps his shoulders square to the net, and he steps towards the middle blocker to 'close' the block

▲ Both blockers jump straight up simultaneously. Their extended arms, and their rigid hands and fingers, form a wall above the net. Their eyes are focused on the hitter

▲ *Ready position: the feet are at least shoulder width apart. The weight is forwards, with the arms in front and at the sides of the body*

▲ *You must move into the correct position quickly. Take a stride with the foot closest to the ball, and try to take the ball inside the knee. Stay low and dig the ball up and forwards*

▲ *The three keys to defensive motion: stay low; stride to the ball; get under the ball. Try to use two hands to dig. The forearm, wrist or fist control depends on the distance of the ball from the body*

Defence

Defence – keeping the ball from hitting the court – is the most difficult technique in volleyball. To defend successfully, you must train the fighting spirit!

Covering

Covering involves moving in relation to a player who is smashing or blocking, in order to play any balls which may rebound or be deflected off the opponents' block and fall near him.

▲ The inside of the left knee gives support and balance. The arms are stretched under the ball for the 'scoop' dig and for back-spin. Dig the ball 6 m (20 ft) high and 3 m (10 ft) away from the net in the centre of the court

▲ 'Half-kneeling' defence requires flexibility. Keep the hips below the ball. From this position you can sprawl, roll or dive to the ball that is further from the body

▲ Side view of defensive position. The weight is forwards, with the heels raised, and the player is ready to move. The arms are in front of the knees, and the knees are in front of the toes. Concentrate hard and be full of confidence and determination

◄ The feet must accelerate quickly to the ball. Move diagonally to intercept the ball. A good dig depends on quick movement; quick movement depends on a quick start

▲ After striding, the ball is still a good way from the body. Thrust forwards from the half-kneeling defensive position and start to sprawl. Keep the arms parallel to the floor and scoop the ball up

▲ Lower your centre of gravity and stride to the ball by pushing off the inside of the foot. The shoulders should be stretched to enlarge the defensive area

▲ Digging power strike. Be aggressive. Show your fighting spirit!

After digging, the hands contact the ▶ ground and soften the landing. The hands push back and the belly slides on the floor. Keep your chin up

Diving technique: used to dig the ball that ▲ is far from the body. Focus the eyes on the ball. One leg kicks up behind the body, while the hands balance

▲ When chasing and pursuing the ball, dive low and far. Use two hands if possible, but one hand may be used

39

Covering the smash

After setting, no.3 in fig. 8 follows the ball and moves in close to the smasher to pick up any balls which rebound from the block. No.6 also performs this function, but stands behind the smasher. No.2 moves to play any balls deflected sideways from the blocks. Nos 1 and 5 cover the rest of the court between them.

All players must stay alert at the moment the ball is hit. Anyone standing rigidly upright will be unable to move quickly to retrieve the ball.

Covering the block

Using the same formation as above, no.6 in fig. 9 stands just behind the 3 m (10 ft) line on the return of service to cover his team's block when the opponents are smashing.

During a rally, no.6 stands near the 3 m (10 ft) line to cover any balls which rebound there, and moves in to cover a block exactly as described above for the smash. He crouches behind the blocking player to play any balls which touch this blocker and fall near him, or any balls tactically placed over or around the blocker.

The front line player who does not block must remember to drop back behind the 3 m (10 ft) line to cover any balls which rebound there.

Starting out

Volleyball is a simple game, requiring great skill, since player contact with the ball is almost instantaneous. When starting to play, or when first introducing the game, do not employ six-a-side immediately; instead, **simplify the game**. Here are some guidelines for teachers and coaches.

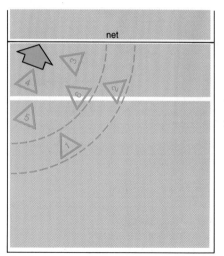

▲ *Fig. 8 Covering the smash*

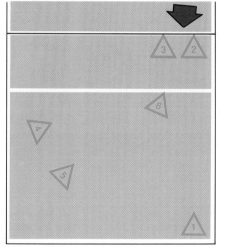

▲ *Fig. 9 Covering the block*

- Use light teaching volleyballs or foam balls – neither of these will hurt beginners' hands. Do *not* use soccer balls, netballs or heavily pimpled plastic balls.
- If a volleyball net is not available, use a clothes line with coloured braids, or skipping ropes attached as court dividers.
- Position the net lengthways down the centre of the gym or sports hall. This provides space for more courts.
- The rope or net should be 2.4–3.0 m (8–10 ft) in height. This ensures passes are high, which **slows the game down** so that beginners have more time to play the ball.
- Introduce competitive games as soon as the volley has been learnt, e.g. 1 v 1, 2 v 2, 3 v 3, etc.
- Rules should be introduced gradually and when appropriate. **Don't be too strict at the outset**.
- Condition games to achieve aims, e.g. each player must play the ball before it is returned over the net.
- In the early stages, don't stop games too often. Instead, work with individuals to improve their personal skills.

- Emphasise the use of basic tactics, e.g. where to serve.
- Try to maximise the extent of practice with a ball.
- Provide practices and drills which help to make the beginner successful.
- It is essential that every player should learn the fundamentals of each position (setter, smasher, etc.), so that they appreciate the demands on each role.
- There should be no early specialisation for players when they first commence playing.

Modified games

Quoit volleyball

- Number of players: 1 v 1 initially.
- Players throw the volleyball over the net (minimum height 1.8 m/6 ft).
- A point is scored for the other side when one player drops the ball.
- Score as for conventional volleyball.
- Size of court: 3 m × 3 m (10 ft × 10 ft).

Heading tennis

- Number of players: 1 v 1 or 2 v 2.

- This game is particularly good for introducing boys to volleyball.
- Players head the ball over a net or rope which is higher than they are.
- A point is scored for the other side if a player allows the ball to drop or if he misheads the ball.
- Eventually, instead of heading the ball, the players catch it just before heading it so that they learn to take the ball near their foreheads with the whole body behind and under the ball.

Juggle ball

- Numbers: as for heading tennis.
- Players now catch the ball, but instead of throwing it back over the net, the player tosses the ball up into the air and then plays it back over the net.
- Again, the emphasis is on taking the ball above head height.
- Scoring: one point to the other side if a player drops or misdirects the ball.

Marathon volleyball

- Number of players: two, three or four.
- No net is required.
- Players volley the ball continuously to one another.

Each group tries to improve on the maximum number of volleys it has achieved.

Basket volleyball

- Number of players: two, three or four, depending on the number of basketball rings available.
- Each player has a number of attempts to volley the ball into a basketball basket.
- The winner is the player with the highest number of successful volleys.
- This can be simplified further by giving one point for every ball which hits the backboard, two points for every ball hitting the ring, and three points for every ball which goes through the basket.

Bounce ball

- Number of players: 1 v 1 or 2 v 2.
- Each player volleys the ball over the net. The opposition must let the ball bounce before volleying it back.
- Thus the ball is easier to play, particularly for youngsters who find that they do not have the strength to play high balls.

Tennis volleyball

- Number of players: 1 v 1.
- Each player volleys the ball back to his partner directly after receiving it – similar to tennis.
- The emphasis is on directing volleys close to the net if the opponent is far back; and on directing deep volleys if the opponent is standing too close to the net.

Doubles

- Number of players: two per side.
- When receiving the ball, a player must pass it to his partner before the ball can be returned over the net.
- The rally continues until one team misplays the ball or until one player does not pass the ball to his partner.

Mini volleyball

- Number of players: 3 v 3.
- A player must again pass to all three players in his side.
- This can be a conditioned game, e.g. the first play must be a dig, or the players must smash on the third play.
- Each player has double the number of ball contacts of the full 6 v 6 game.

- The smaller court helps develop movement, increasing the length of rallies and thus making for a more exciting game.
- Two of the three are 'net' players; the third is the main defence/reception player.

Midi volleyball

- This is a progression from mini volleyball. It is played by two teams each consisting of four players, with two substitutes per team.
- Net length: 2.10 m (6.9 ft).
- Size of the court: 9 m × 6 m (30 ft × 20 ft).
- Midi volleyball helps in the transition from mini to full six-a-side volleyball. Both technically and tactically, it is a large step up from mini volleyball. The demands on the players increase enormously.
- With three of the four players playing as attackers, the server is the only back court player.

Do not play **mass volleyball**, or some individuals will never touch the ball, and the opportunity for skills to develop will be reduced.

Officials and discipline

In competitive play the following officials are required: first referee, second referee, scorer and four linesmen. In simple, recreational games, one referee and a scorer will be adequate.

The first referee

All decisions of the referee are final, and he has absolute authority over the game and all other officials.

The referee uses a whistle to signify the beginning and end of games, a point, change of service, foul, etc. In top-class play a referee's platform is also essential, similar to that used in tennis, only higher.

The referee warns any player who:

● disputes with the referee or an opponent
● shouts on court, with the intention of distracting or intimidating the officials or opposition

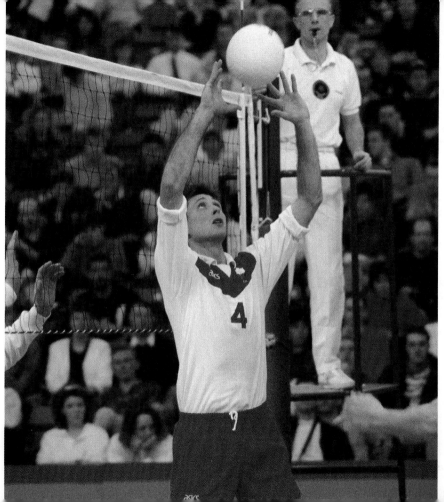

- intentionally delays the game in any way.

The referee gives a personal warning to players who repeat the offence. A personal warning is recorded by the scorer and penalised by loss of point or service. After two warnings, or for any particularly unpleasant behaviour, the offending player is disqualified, but he may be replaced by a substitute.

The second referee

The second referee places himself on the opposite side of the court to the first referee, and assists him in every way.

The second referee notes the players' positions at the start of the game, authorises substitution, and keeps a check on all 'time-outs' (*see* page 12). He draws the first referee's attention to unsporting play, and blows his whistle for faults concerning:

- crossing of the centre line
- crossing of the line of attack ('spiking line')
- contacts with the net.

The scorer

The scorer positions himself opposite the first referee, and takes note of the score. He also notes all time-outs, substitutions and any other interruptions.

Before the set begins the scorer takes the names of the players, substitutes, captains and coaches. He receives from the captains or coaches the positions of the players on court, and ensures that the rotation order is kept during the match.

The linesmen

If four linesmen are available, they are placed at the four corners of the court. If only two are available, they are placed at diagonal corners, away from the service areas.

The linesmen are under the orders of the referee, who can amend their decisions. They raise their flags when the ball is out, and point them down to indicate when the ball is in court.

Duties of players

Every player must know the rules and keep strictly to them. During the game a player can only address the referee through the captain of his team.

The following offences by players, substitutes and coaches are punished:

- persistently addressing the officials about their decisions
- making unpleasant remarks to officials
- committing unpleasant acts or actions tending to influence the officials' decisions
- making personal remarks to or acting unpleasantly towards opponents
- deliberate coaching during the game from anyone outside the courts other than the coach (except during time-out).

Sanctions are as follows:

- for a slight fault: a single warning
- for a serious fault: a personal warning recorded on the score sheet, which automatically entails the loss of a point or exchange of service (whichever is applicable). If the offence is repeated, the referee may disqualify the player for the set or match.

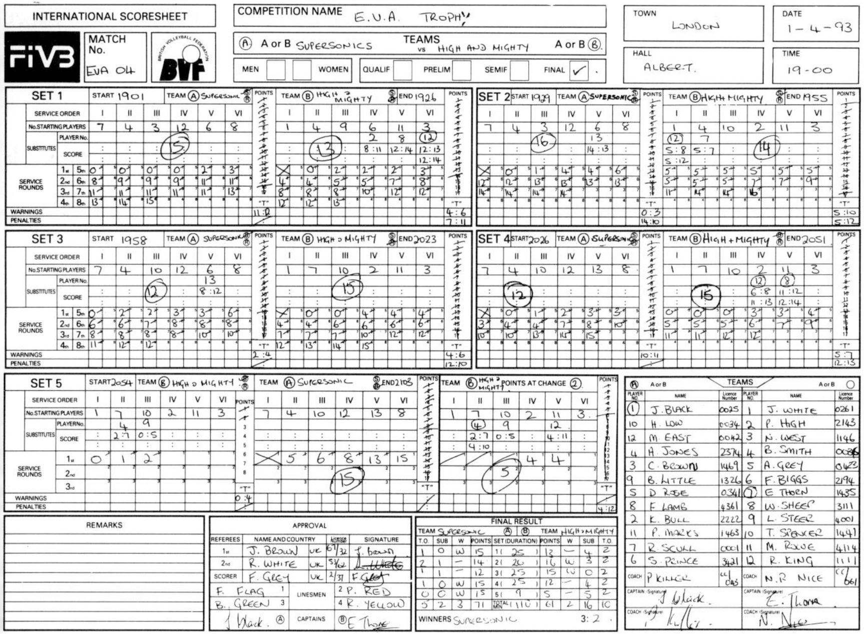

INTERNATIONAL SCORESHEET
COMPETITION NAME E.U.A. TROPHY
TOWN LONDON
DATE 1-4-93
MATCH No. EUA 04
Ⓐ A or B SUPERSONICS TEAMS vs HIGH AND MIGHTY A or B Ⓑ
HALL ALBERT
TIME 19-00
MEN WOMEN QUALIF PRELIM SEMIF FINAL ✓
SET 1 START 1901 END 1926
SET 2 START 1929 END 1955
SET 3 START 1958 END 2023
SET 4 START 2026 END 2051
SET 5 START 2054 END 2103
REMARKS
APPROVAL
REFEREES 1st J. BROWN UK 2nd R. WHITE UK
SCORER F. GREY UK
LINESMEN 1 F. FLAG 2 P. RED 3 B. GREEN 4 R. YELLOW
CAPTAINS Ⓐ J. Black Ⓑ E. Thorne
FINAL RESULT
TEAM SUPERSONIC Ⓐ Ⓑ TEAM HIGH + MIGHTY
WINNERS SUPERSONIC 3:2
TEAMS
Ⓐ J. BLACK, H. LOW, M. EAST, H. JONES, C. BROWN, B. LITTLE, D. ROSE, F. LAMB, K. BULL, P. MARKS, R. SCULL, S. PRINCE; COACH P. KILLER
Ⓑ J. WHITE, P. HIGH, N. WEST, B. SMITH, A. GREY, F. BIGGS, E. THORN, W. SHEEP, L. STEER, T. SPENCER, M. ROWE, R. KING; COACH N. R. NICE

▲ *Fig. 10 A completed score sheet*

Management and leadership

Managers, coaches and captains have team discipline as their responsibility.

The coach cannot interfere with the referee's decisions.

The coach may request time-out and substitution. When the game is interrupted for a time-out, the coach has the right to speak to players, but may not enter the court.

The captain is the direct manager of the team on court, and the only member of the team who may address the officials. If the team has no manager or coach, the captain assumes all duties.

Scoring

Points

The serving team scores a point when:

- the ball touches the ground inside the opponent's court
- the opponents have played the ball more than three times consecutively

- an opponent holds or pushes the ball
- the ball touches an opponent below the knee
- an opponent touches the ball two consecutive times
- an opponent touches the net
- an opponent reaches over the net to play the ball, except to block or hinder a player of the serving team
- an opponent reaches under the net and touches the ball or any opposing player when the ball is in play on that side
- an opponent completely crosses the centre line
- at the moment of service, the opposing team commits a fault of position, e.g. after winning service has not rotated clockwise
- a returned ball crosses or touches the net outside the antennae which determine the width of the court
- a returned ball goes out of court, passes under the net, touches an object outside the court, or is returned by a player aiding himself with any object as support
- an opposing back court player in the attack area incorrectly returns the ball (*see* page 7)

- an opponent receives a personal warning
- the opponents delay the game in a persistent manner
- the opponents illegally replace a player
- the opponents prolong the interruption of the game for more than 30 seconds.

In every set except the deciding one, only the serving team can score points. If the non-serving team wins a rally, it gains the right to serve rather than a point.

In the deciding set, if the serving team wins a rally it scores a point and continues to serve; if the receiving team wins the rally, it gains the right to serve **and** scores a point.

The set

A set is won by the team that first scores 15 points, with a minimum lead of two points. If the score reaches 14–14, play is continued until a two-point lead is reached (e.g. 16–14 or 17–15). However, a point limit is reached at 17, i.e. if the score is 16–16, the team scoring the

next point wins the set with only a one-point lead.

In the deciding set, should the score be a 14–14 tie, play continues until a two-point lead is gained by one team.

A match is won by the team that gains three sets, i.e. each match is the best of five sets.

Beach volleyball

Beach volleyball is very similar to the conventional game, but it is played on a sand court. There are two match formats.

Format A
- Played over one set only.
- A team wins the set and the match by scoring 15 points, with a lead of two points.
- In the event of a 16–16 tie, the team scoring the seventeenth point wins the set and the match with a lead of only one point.

Format B

● Best of three sets.

● A team wins the first two sets by scoring 12 points, with a lead of two points, and wins the match by winning two sets.

● In the event of a 14–14 tie, the team scoring the fifteenth point wins the set with a lead of only one point.

● In the case of a 1–1 tie in sets, a team must win the third and deciding set by scoring 15 points, with a lead of two points. The deciding set is played as a tie-break, when a point is scored whenever a team wins a rally.

The English Volleyball Association has recognised the increasing popularity of beach volleyball and each year licenses a number of tournaments. The FIVB organises the annual World Beach Volleyball Championships, which take place in venues as far afield as Australia, the USA, Japan and Brazil.

▲ *Beach volleyball*

47

Index